About

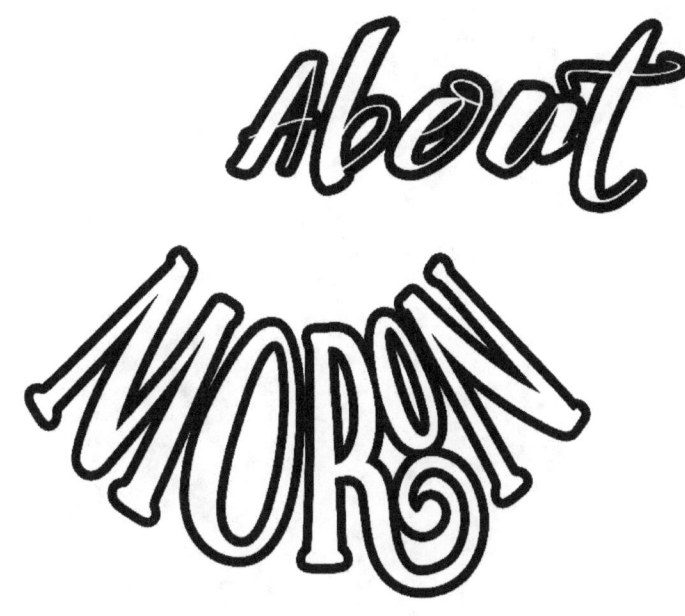

MORON

Outstanding Swear Word To Color

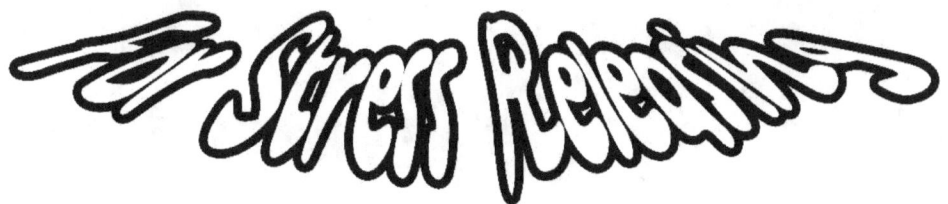

For Stress Releasing

Ja Millie Hawthorn

Happy Coloring!

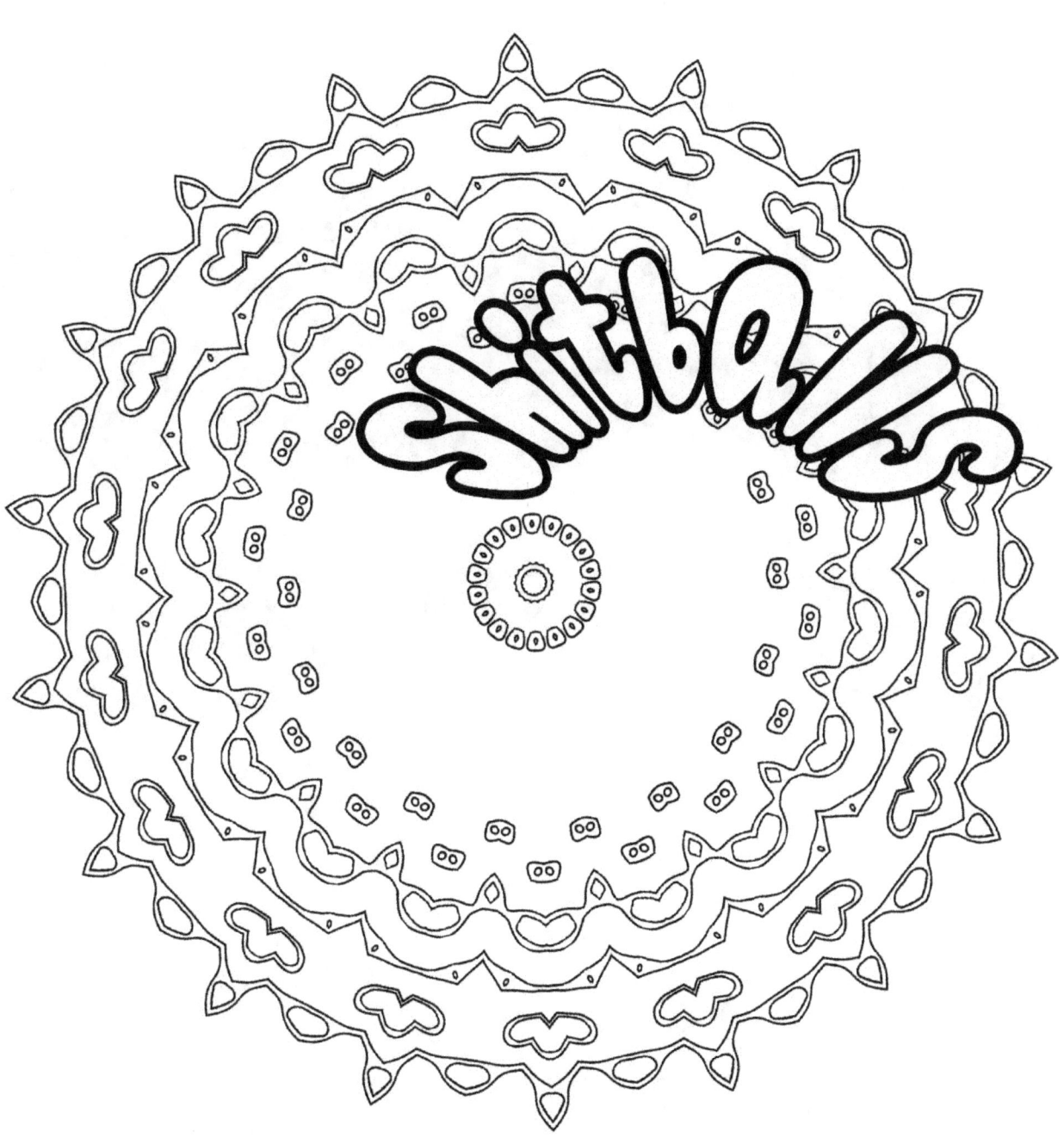

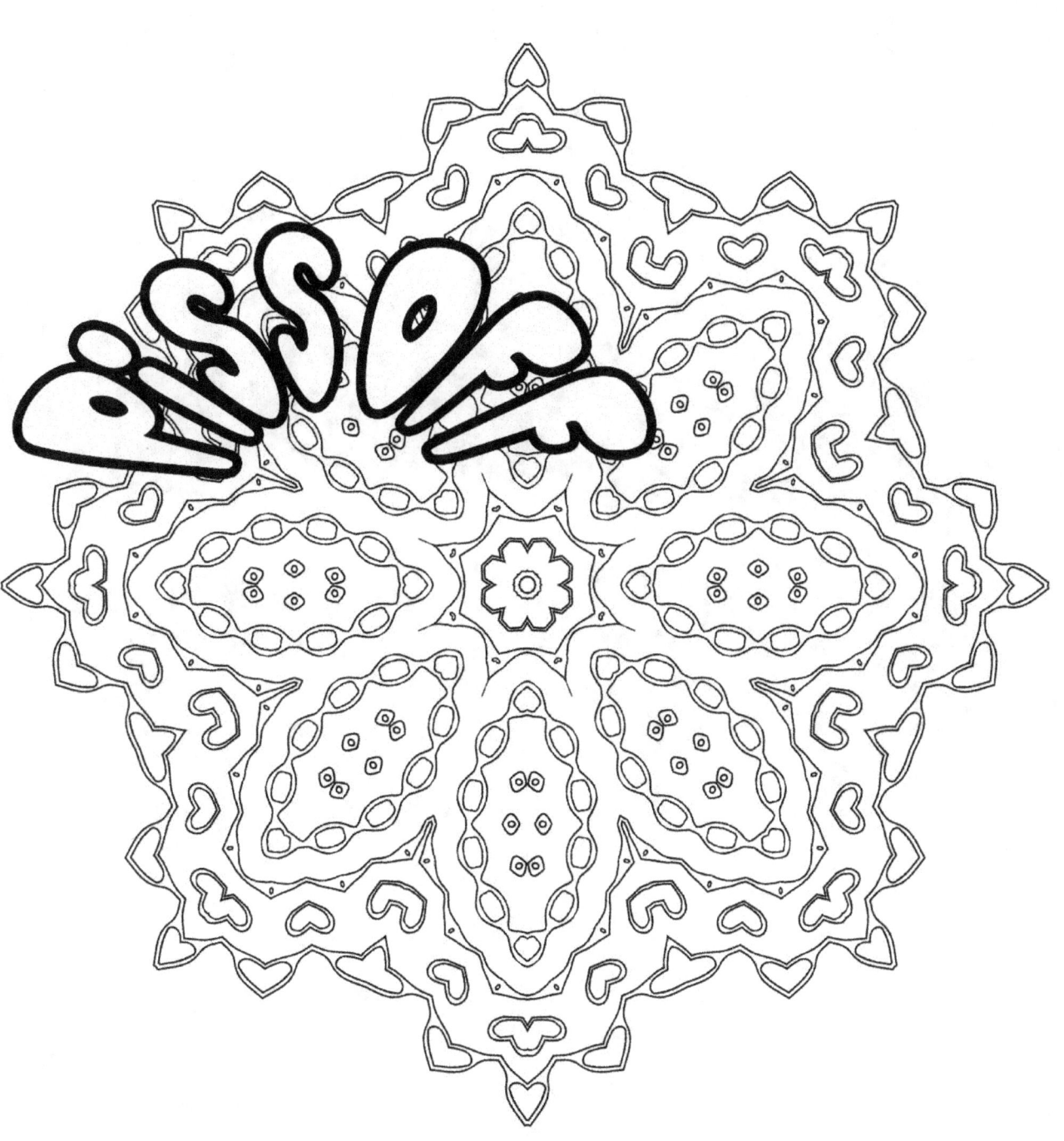

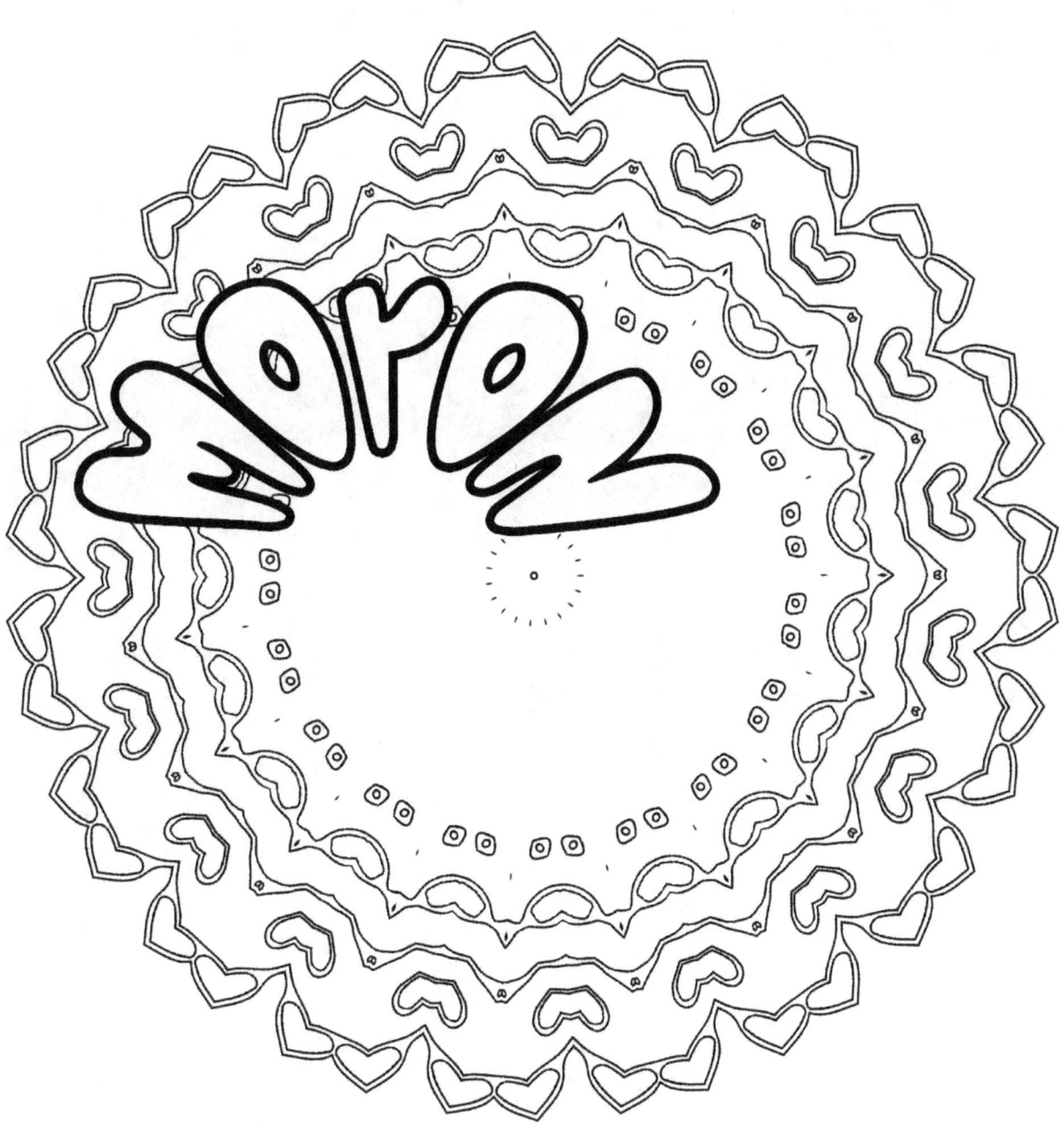

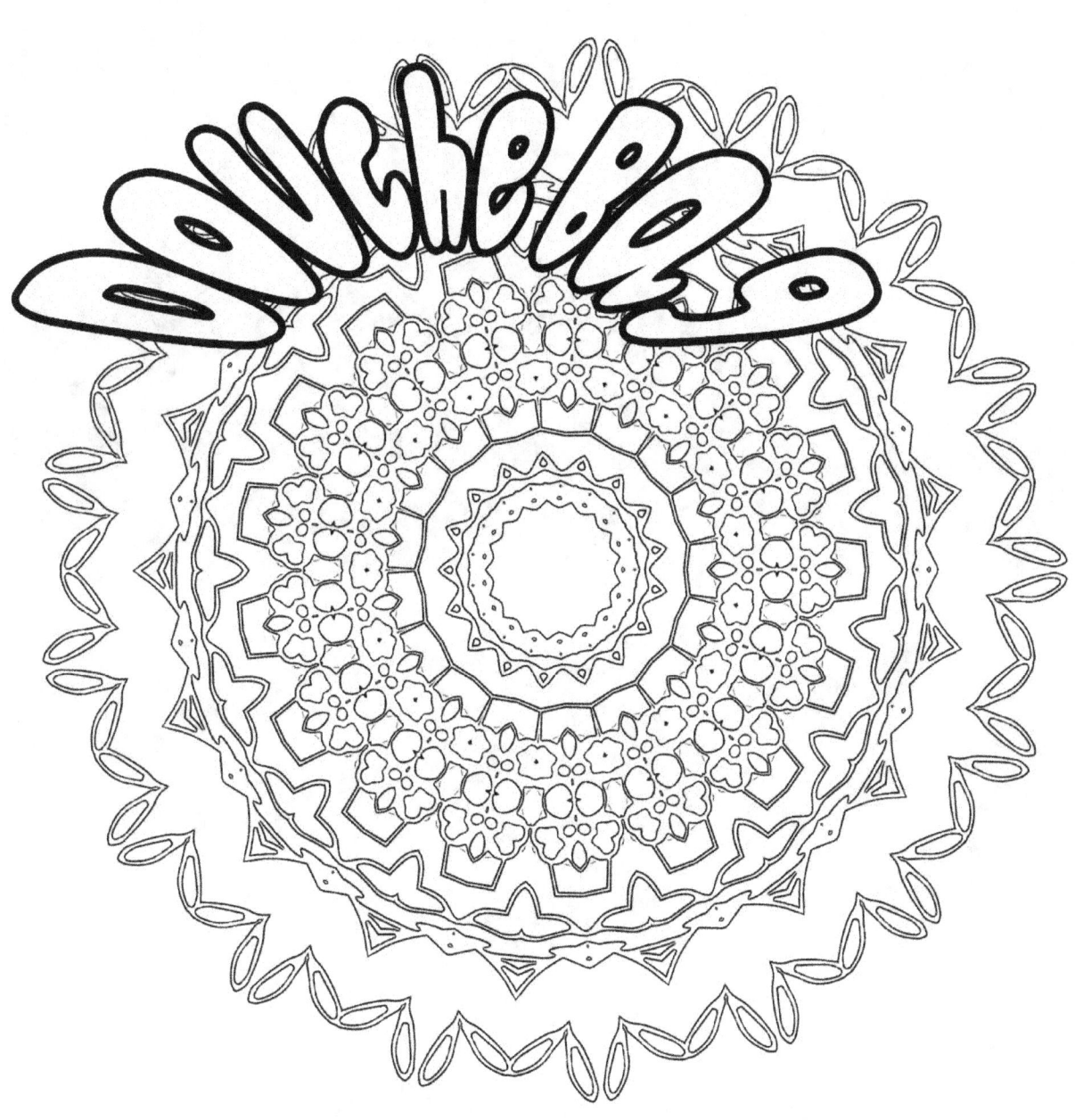

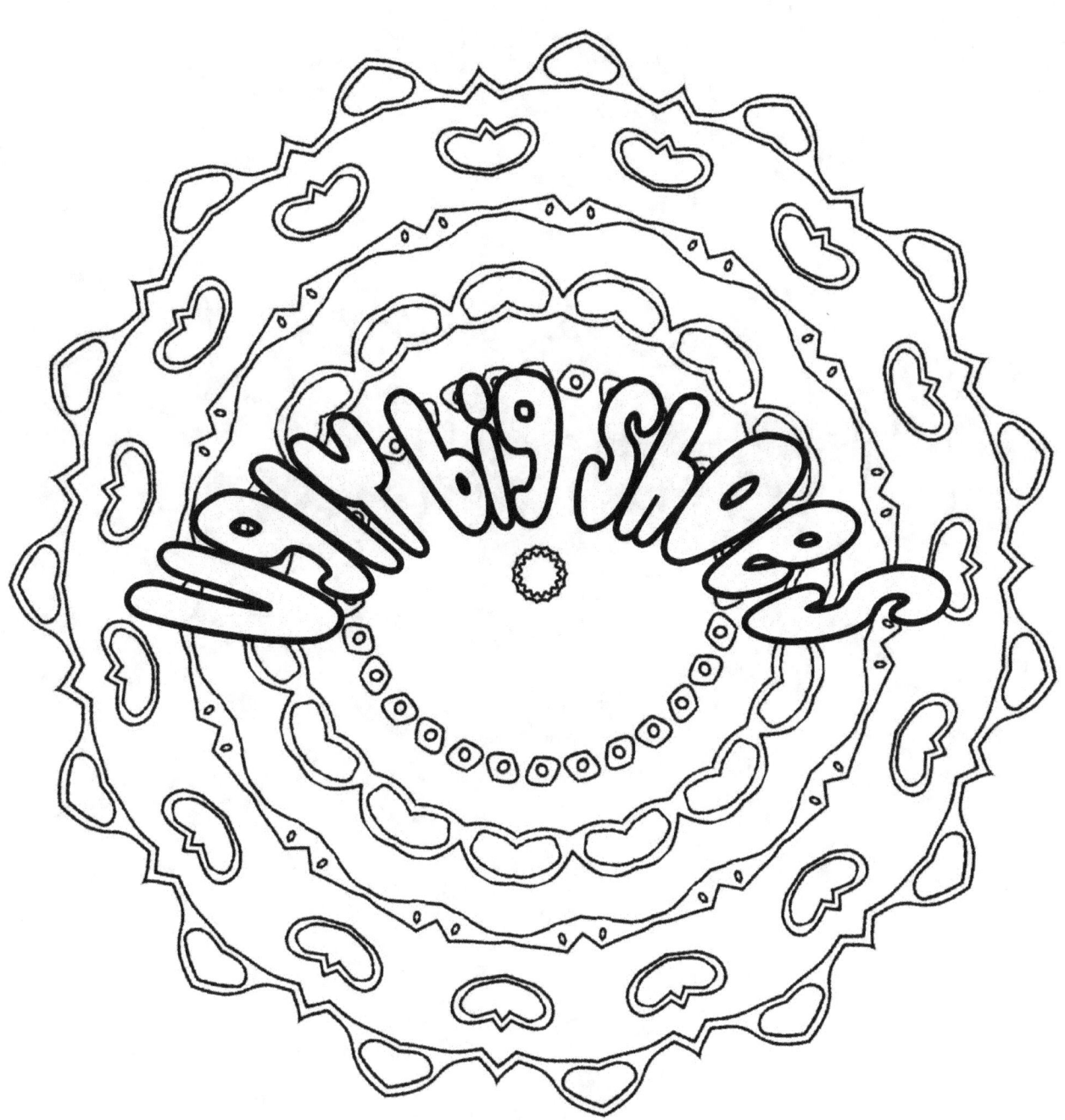

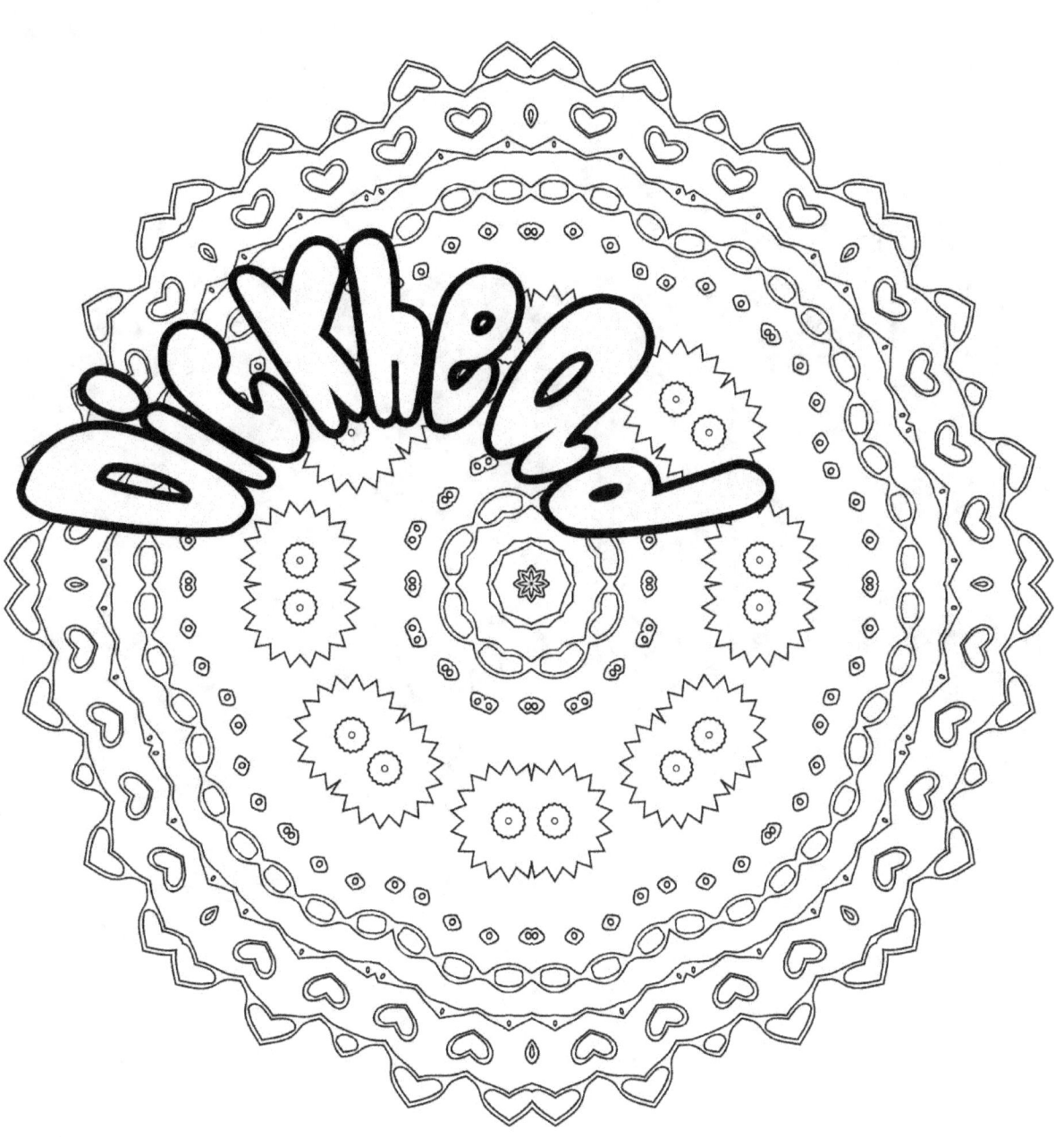

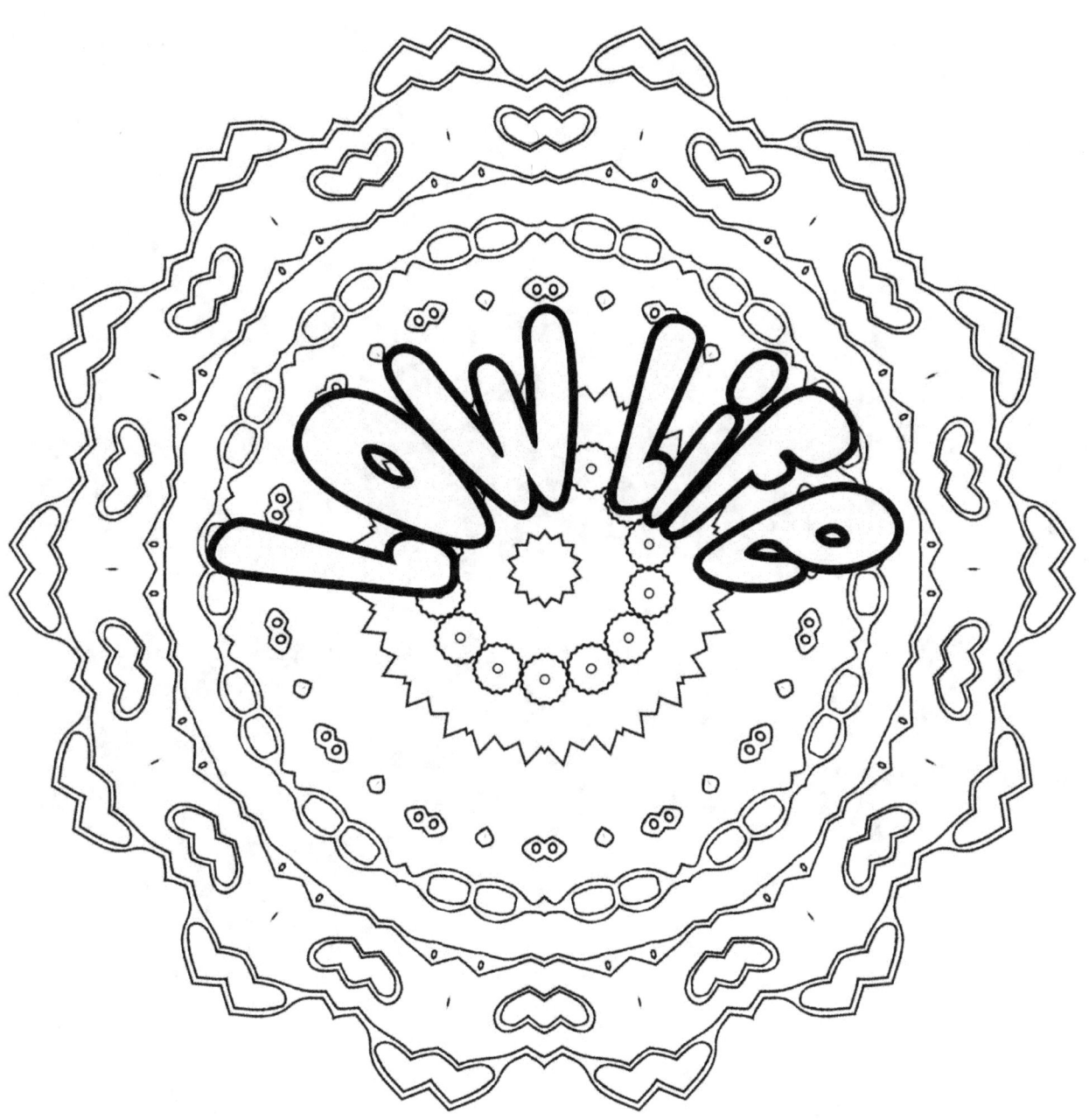

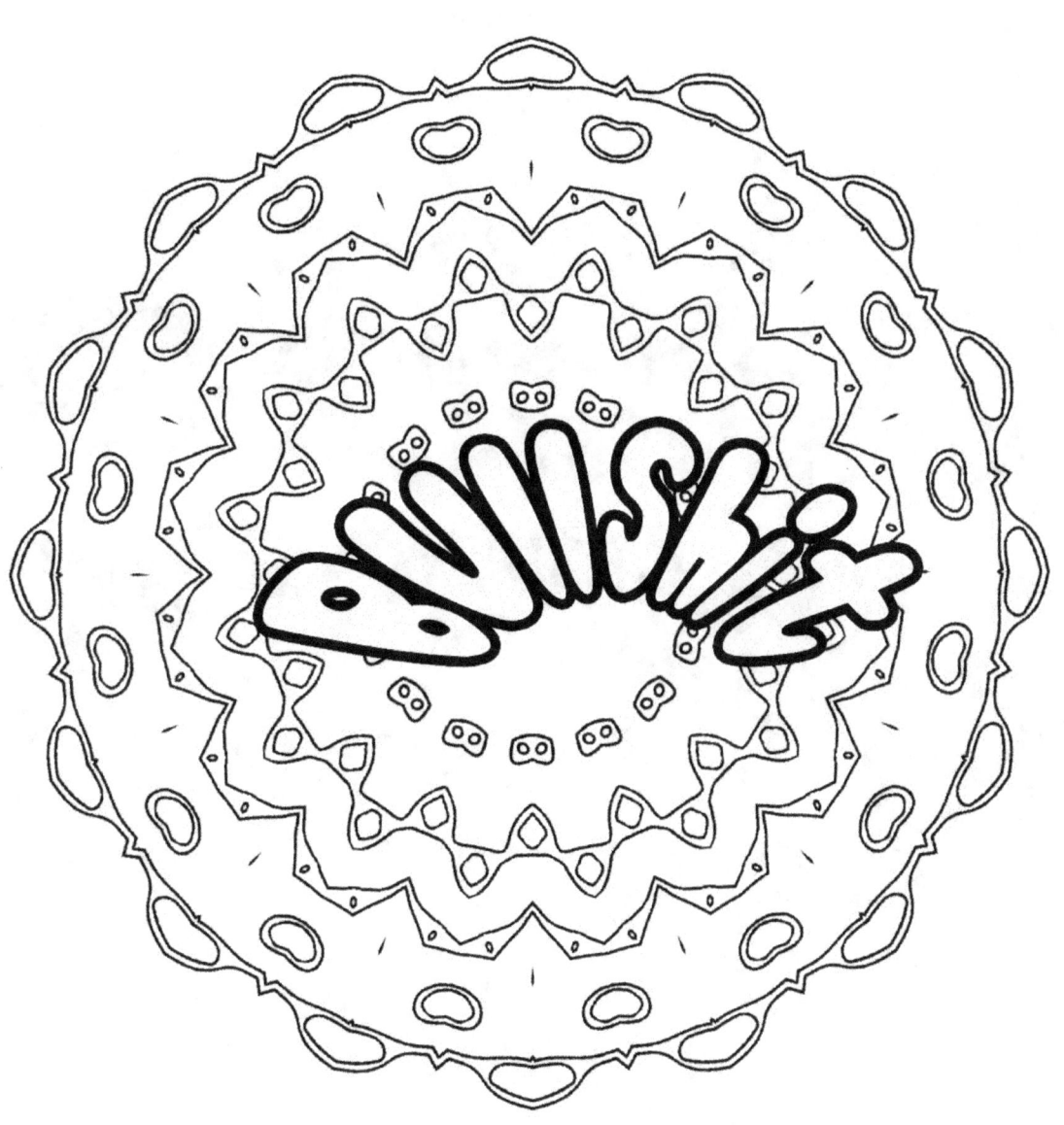

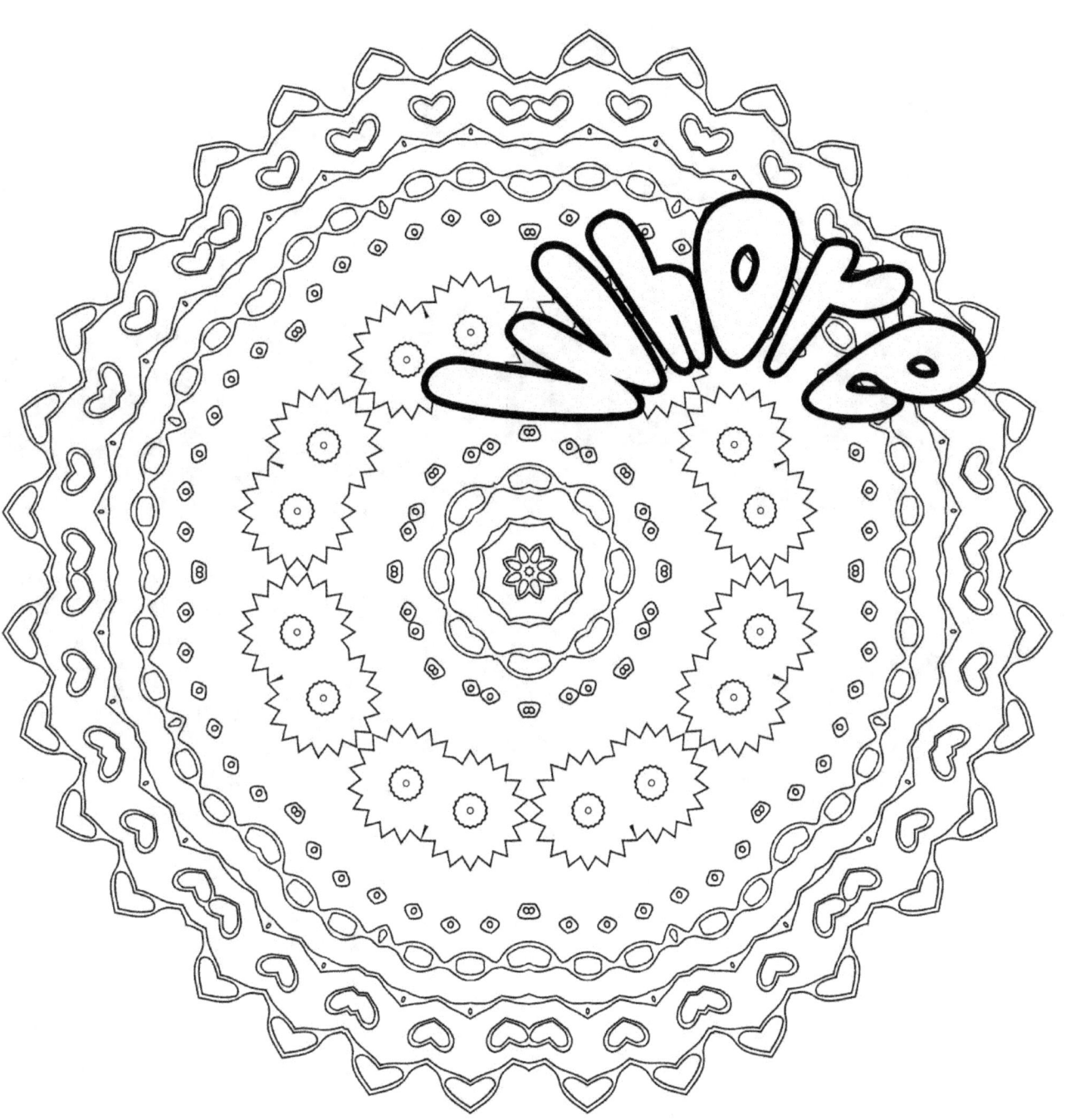

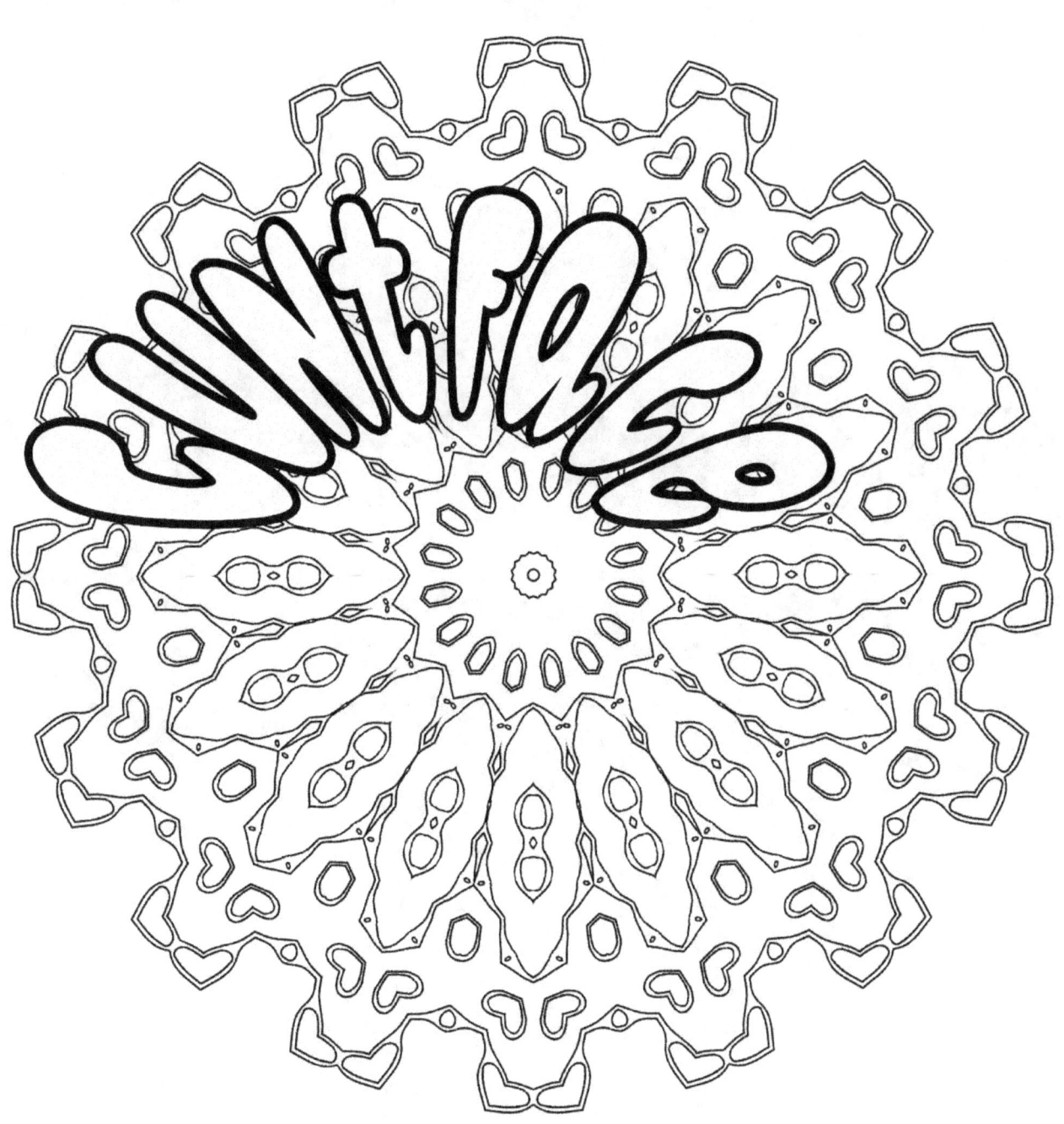

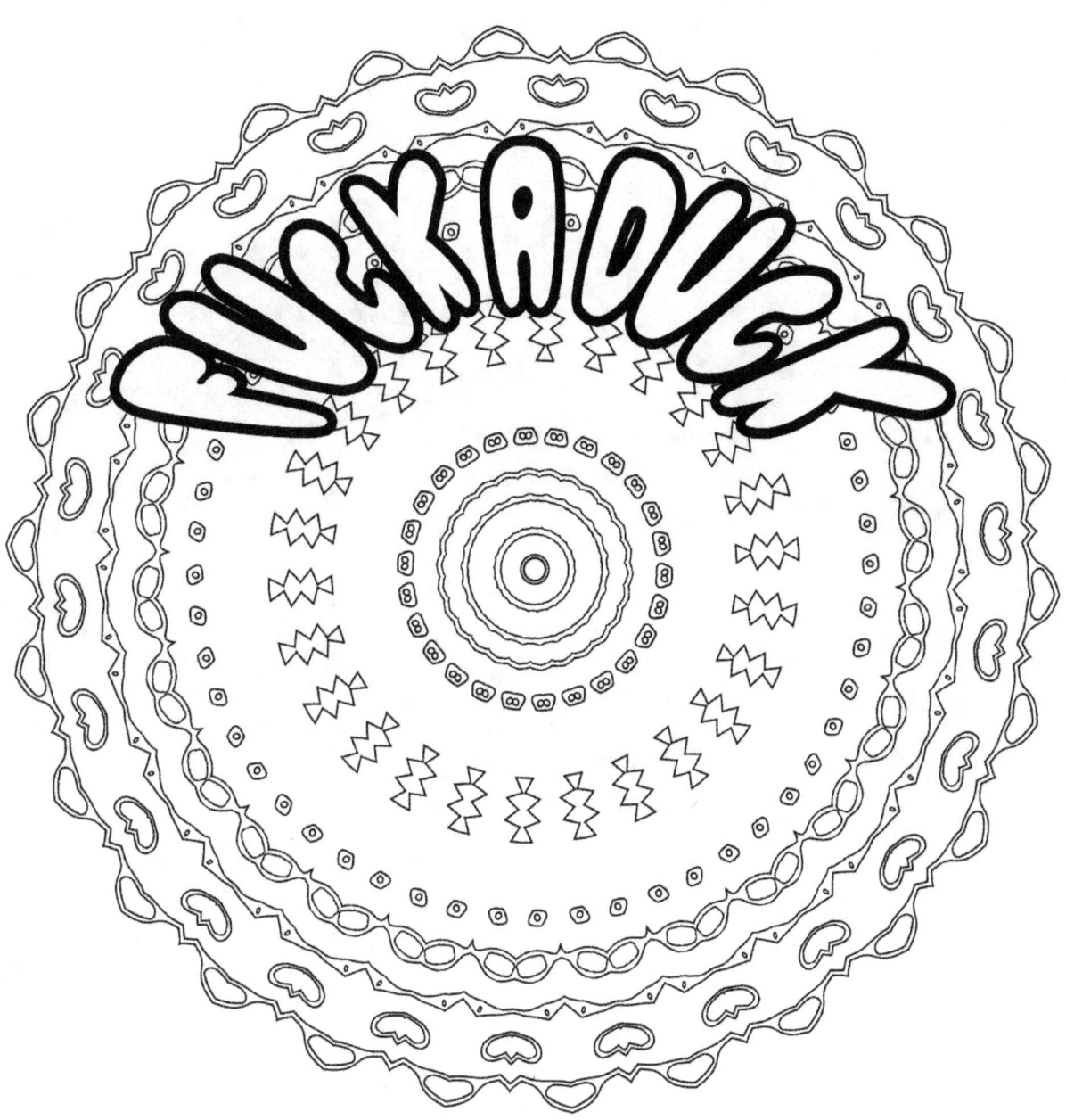

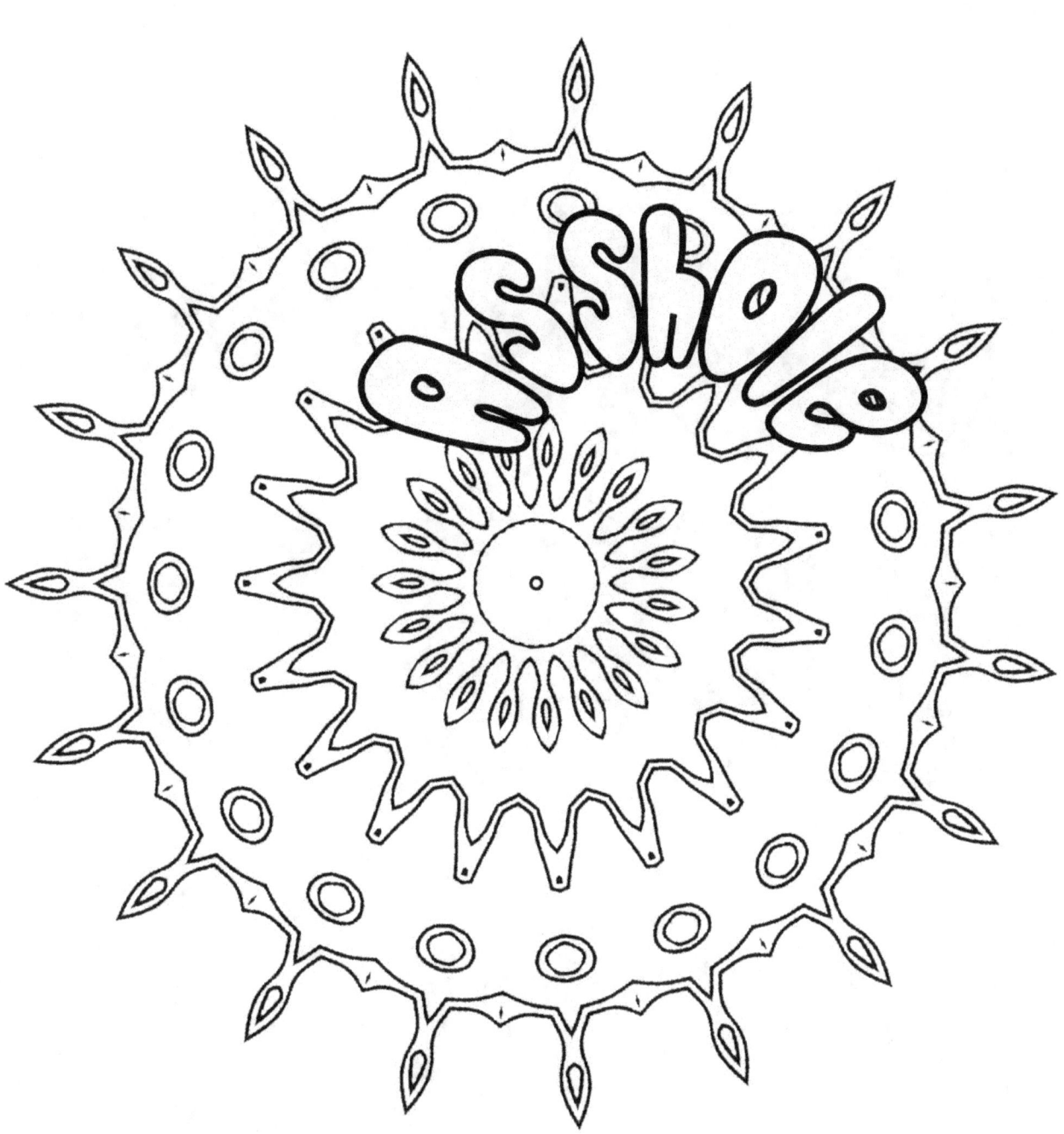

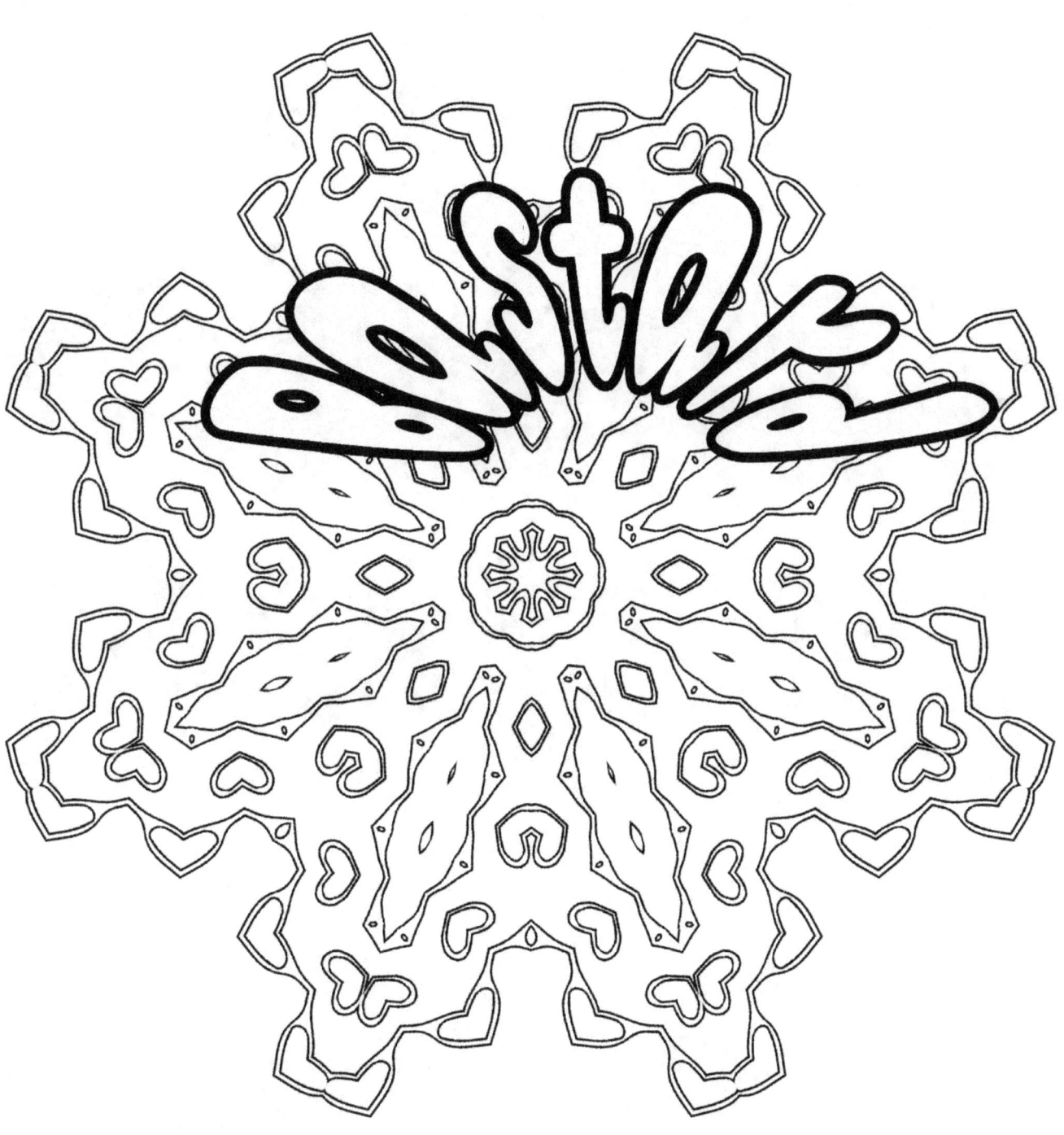

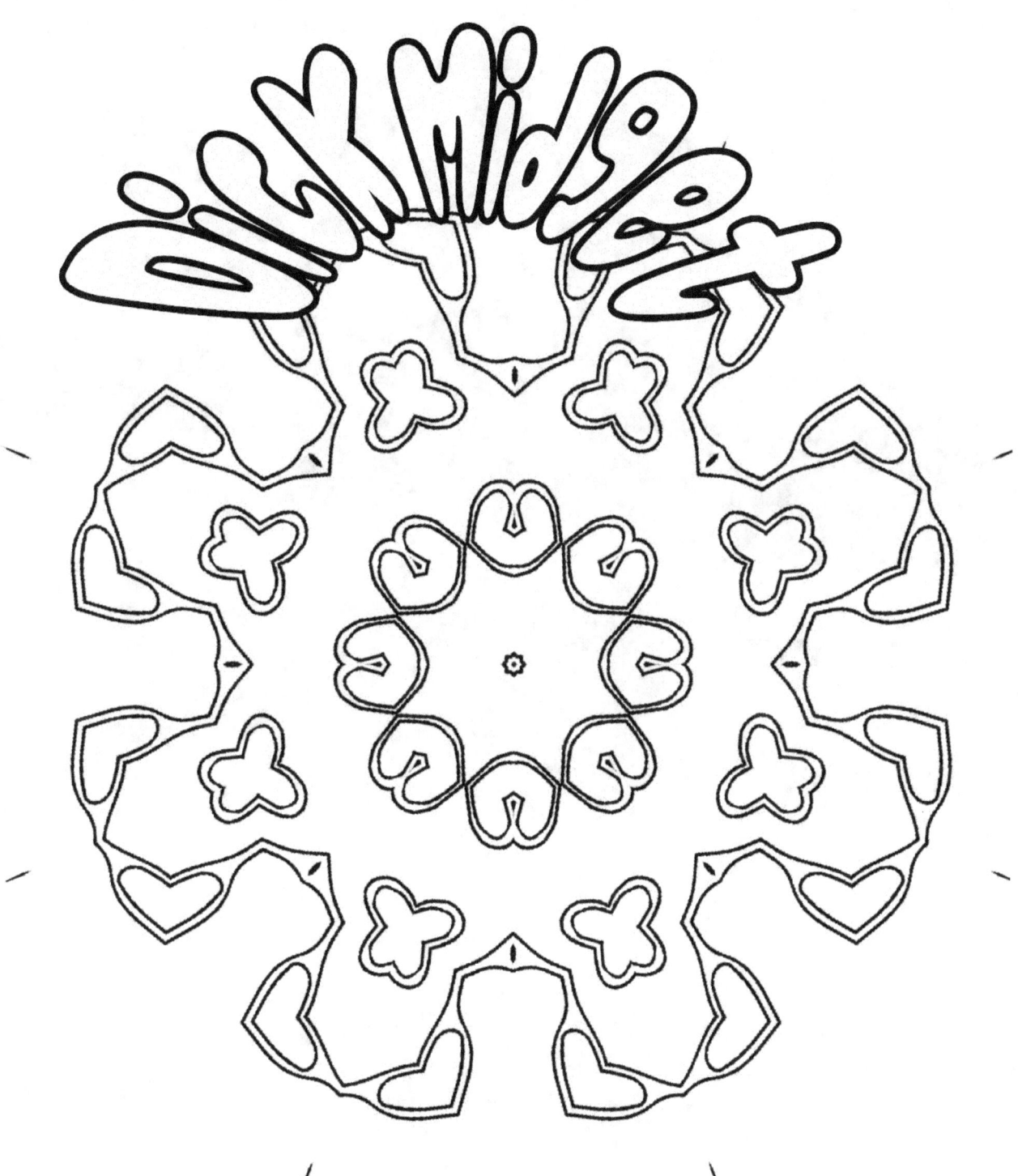

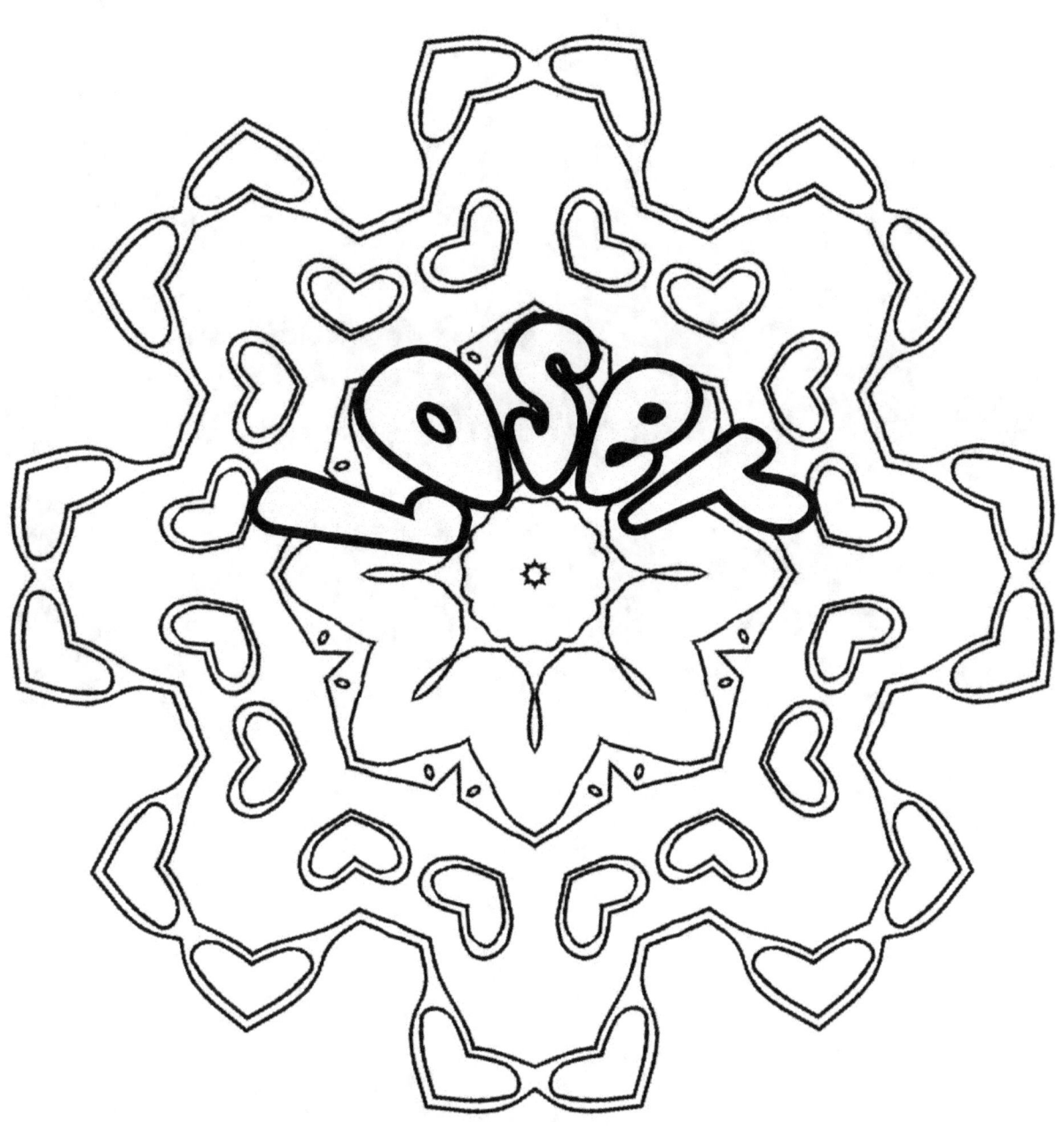

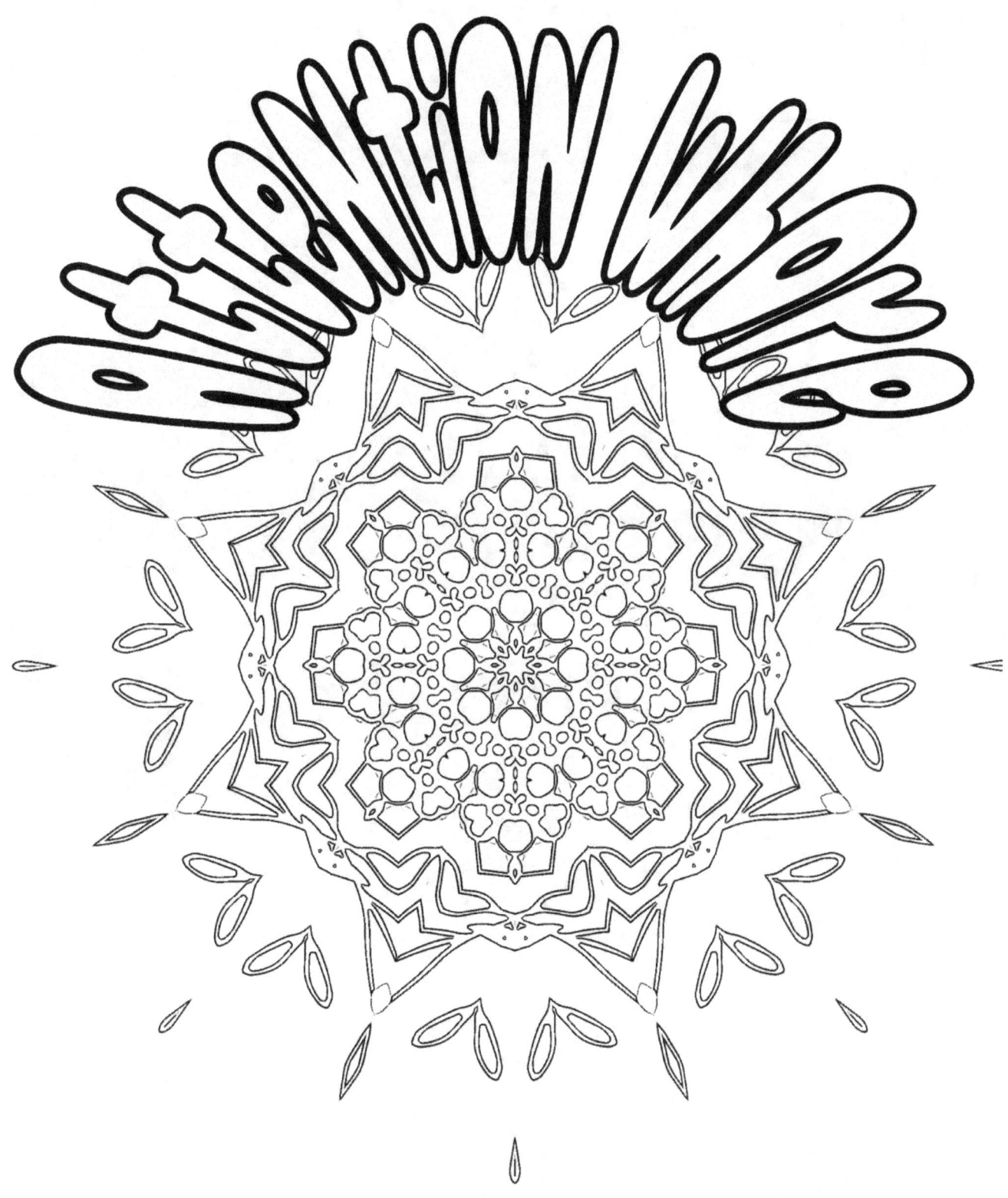

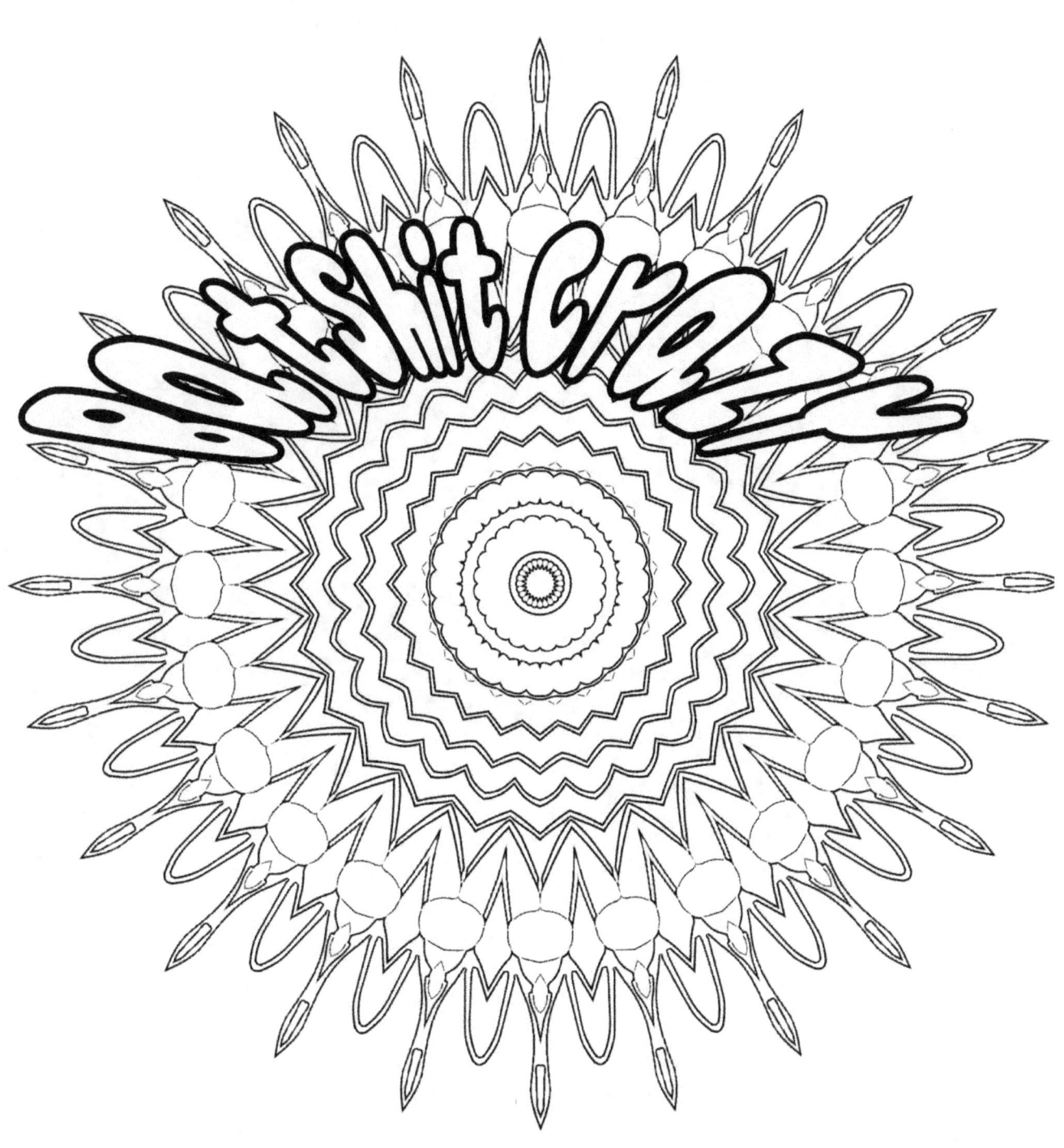

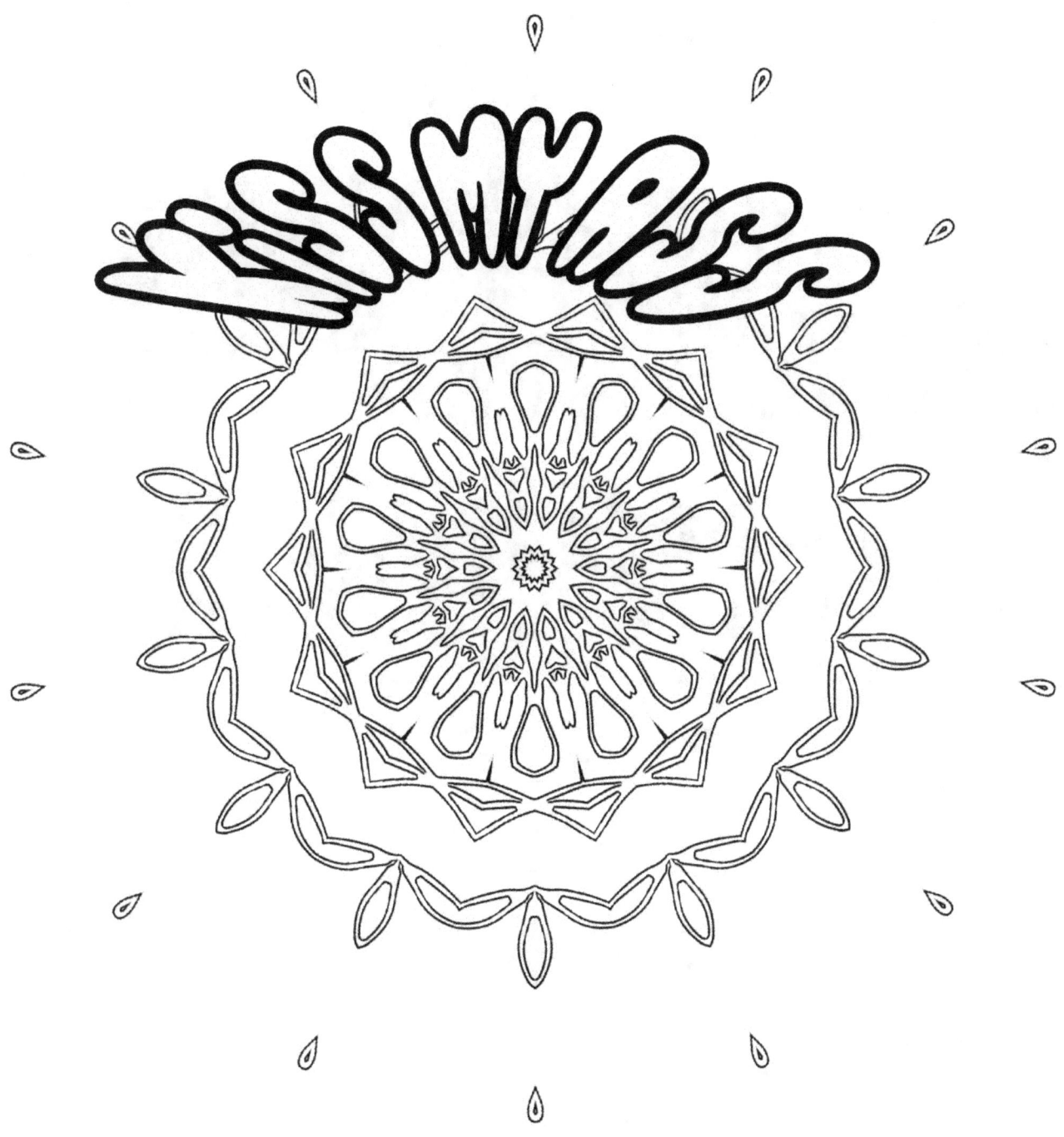

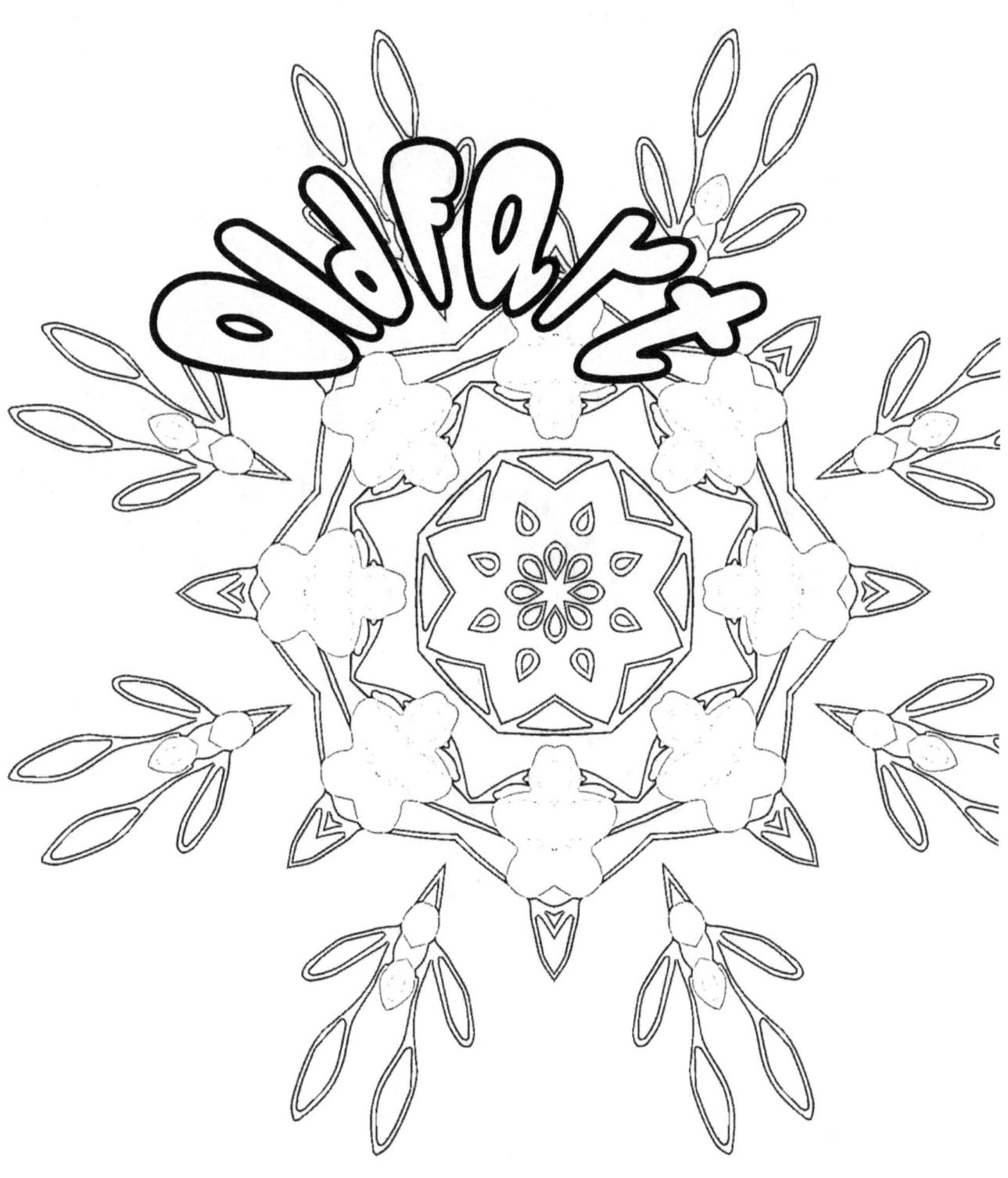

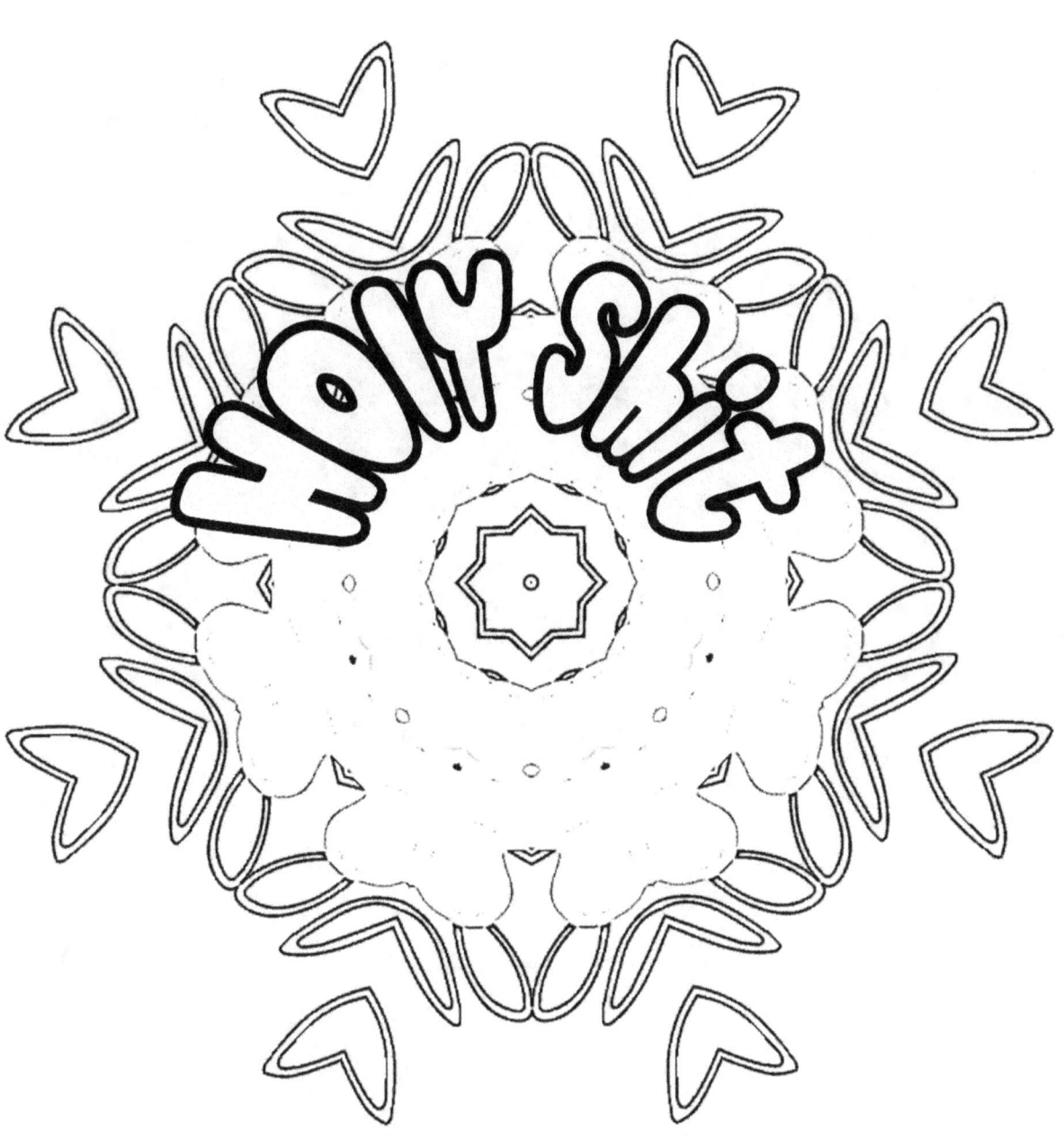

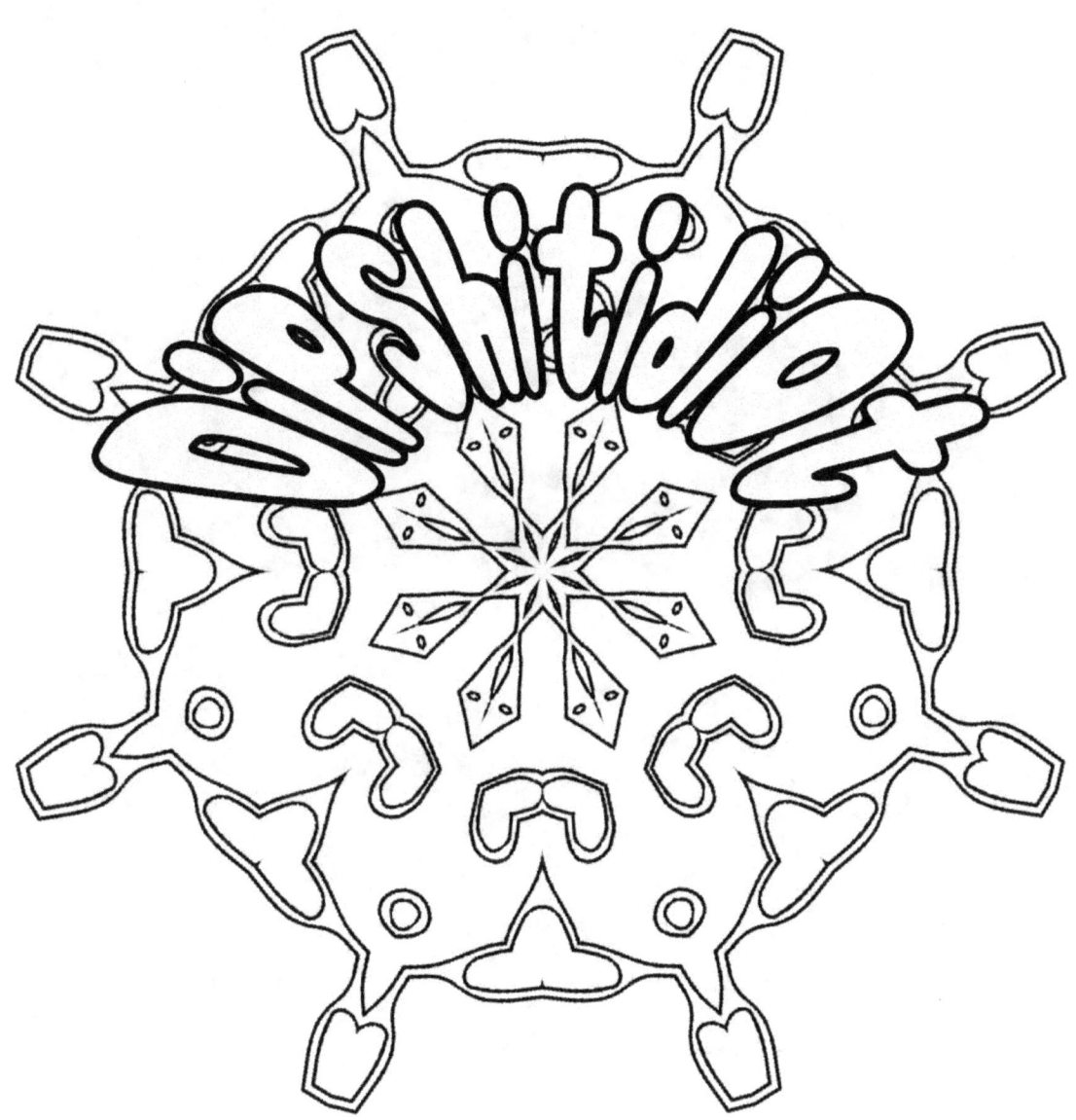

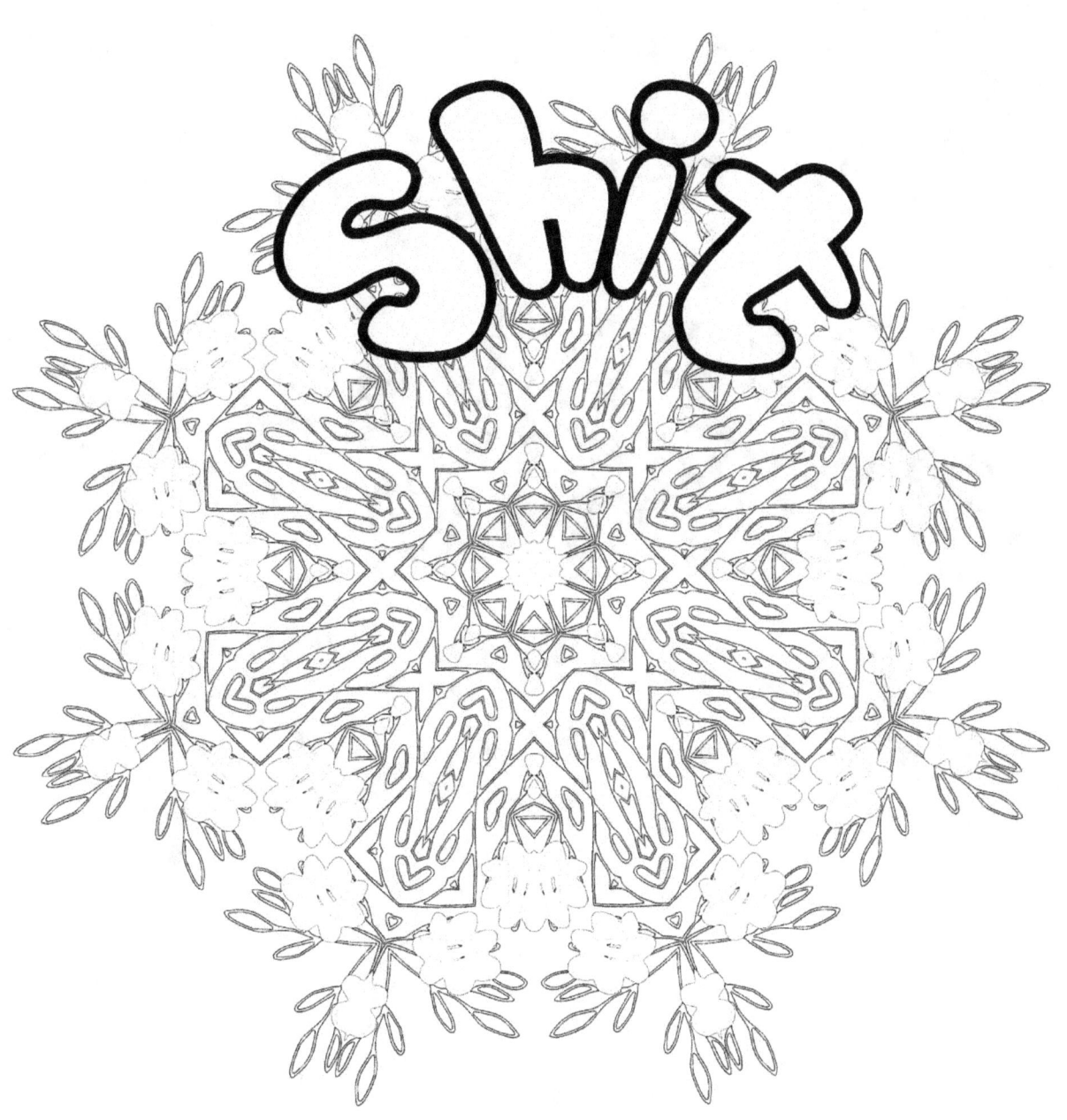

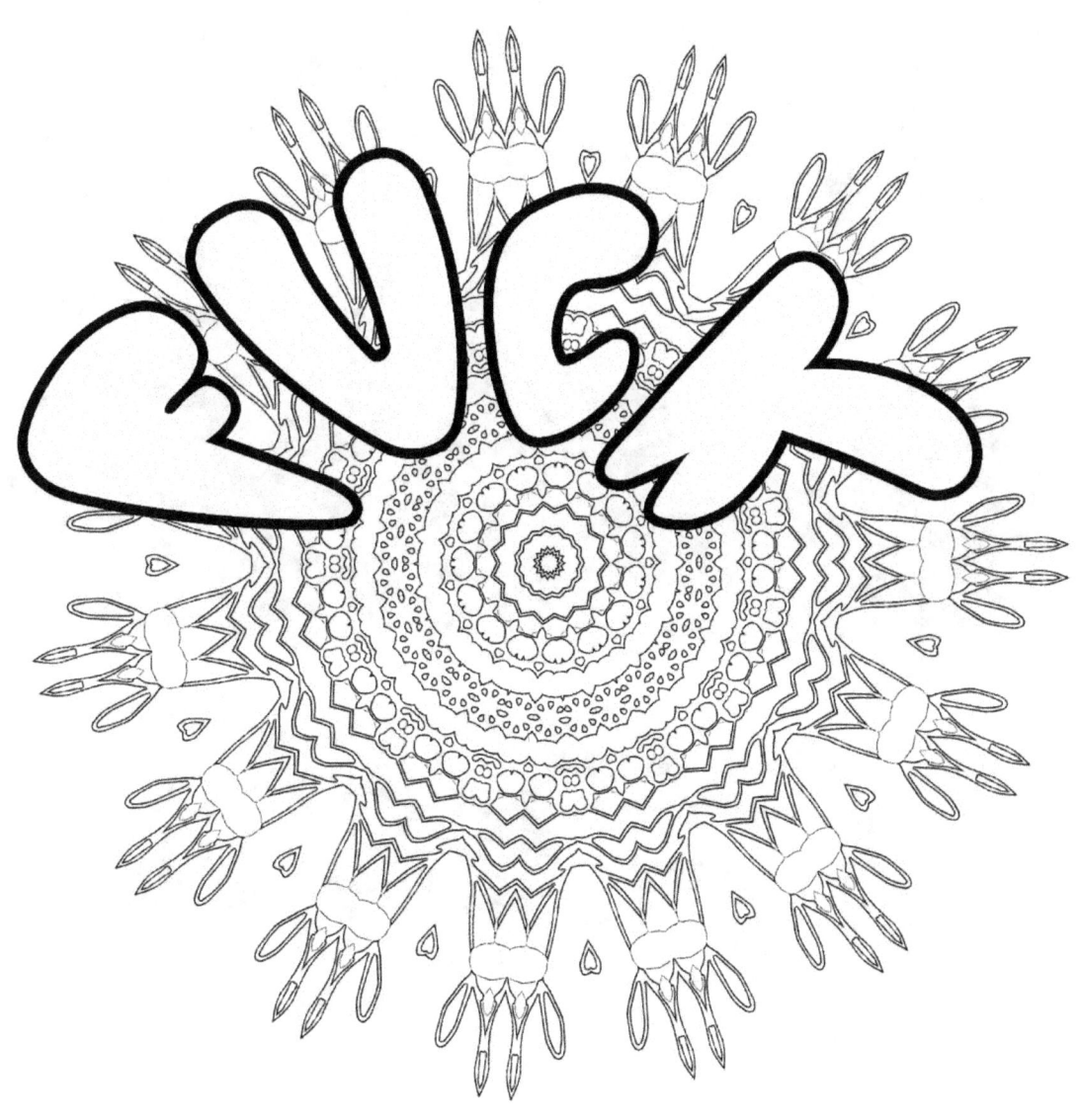

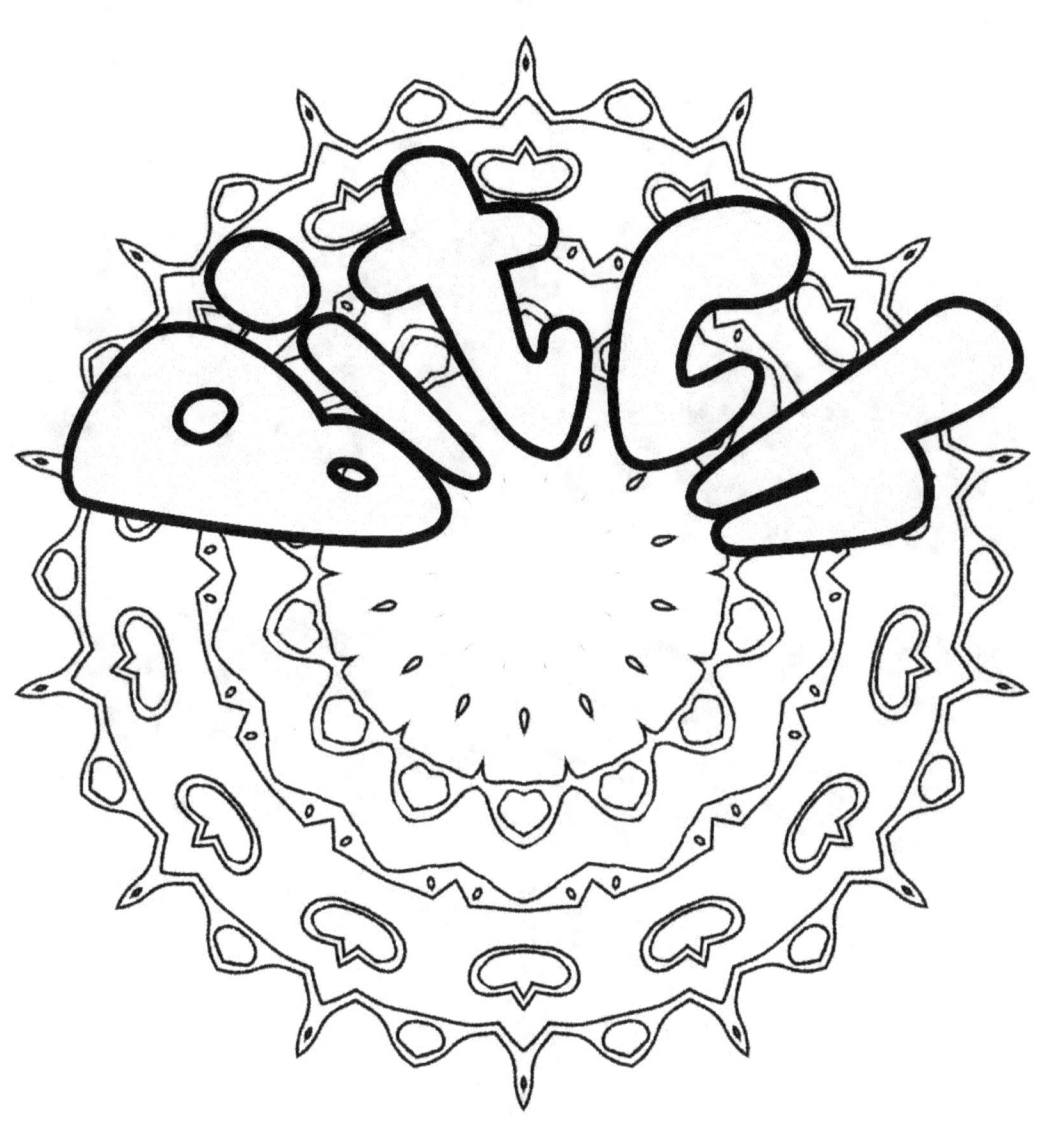

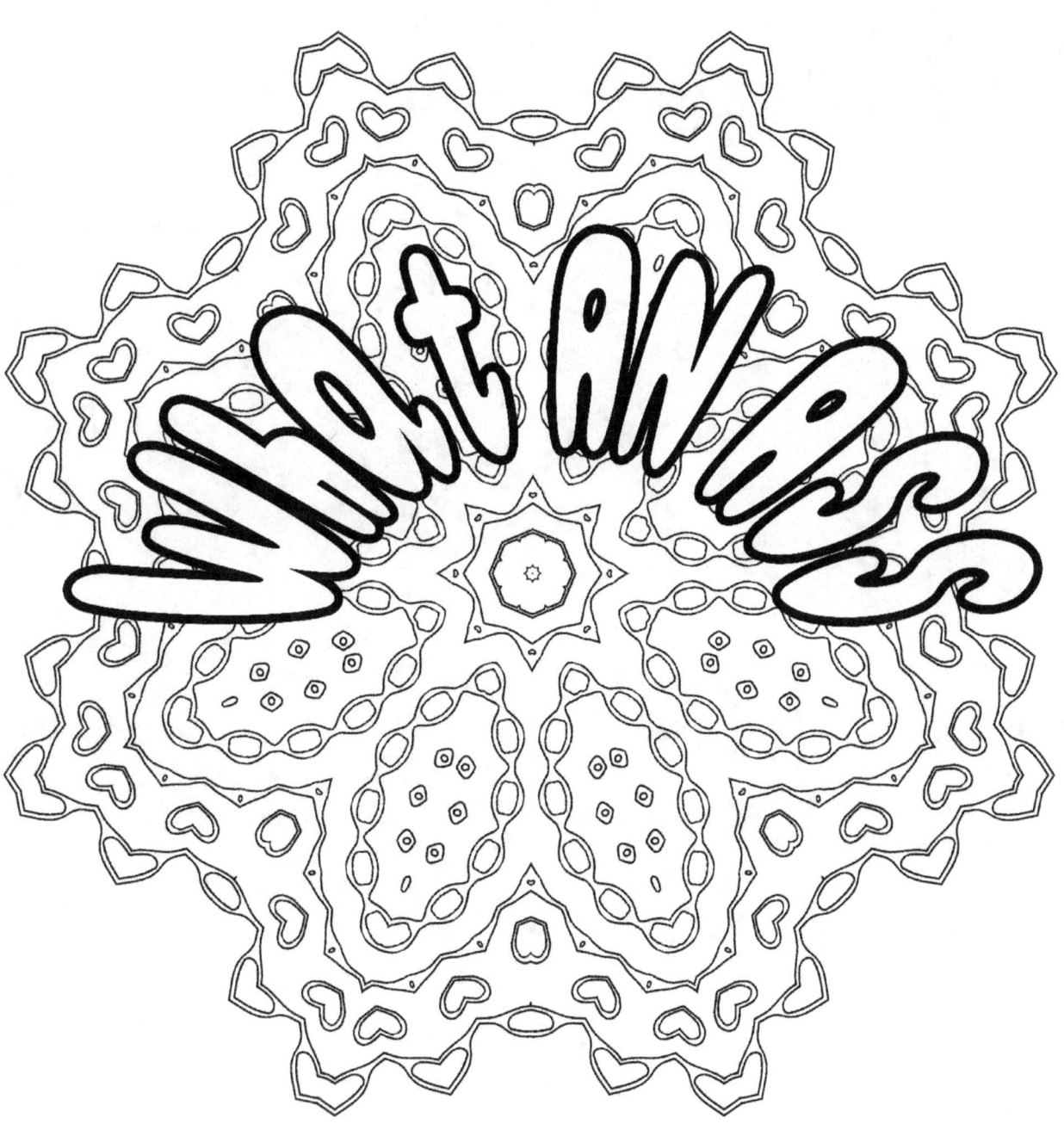

www.ingramcontent.com/pod-product-compliance
Lightning Source LLC
Chambersburg PA
CBHW081747170526
45167CB00009B/3952